PrintHouse Books Presents.

The Party Life.
179 Cocktail Recipe's.
2nd Edition

ANTWAN 'ANT' BANK$

VIP INK Publishing Group, Inc.

© 2012, by Antwan Anderson

PrintHouse Books, Atlanta, GA.

Printhousebooks.com

VIP INK Publishing Group, Incorporated

All rights reserved. No parts of this book may be reproduced in any way, shape, or form or by any means without permission in writing from the publisher or author, except by a reviewer.

Cover art designed by ANT BANK$.

Published;   9-21-2012

Paperback isbn – 978-0-9886428-2-9

Library of Congress Cataloging-in-Publication Data

Antwan'Ant'Bank$

1.Drink Recipes 2.Cooking Recipe's
3.Bartender's guide
4.Antwan 'Ant' Bank$

Printed in the USA.

The following collection of spirits; were some of my favorites to mix for the thousands of customers that I served as a bartender back in my 20's. During 1995 - 1996, I worked as a bartender in several Las Vegas Clubs and had a damn good time doing it! I've included a few recipes I picked up from fellow bartenders, some from customers and most I've learned from bartending school.

Mixology is an art and if mastered one can make a really good living serving spirits and conversing with the people you serve at your bar. If you're a bartender looking for some new drinks or you're just someone interested in mixing up some new drinks in your kitchen. This book of spirits is for you. Welcome to the Party Life and remember to drink responsibly.

Dedicated to the Party people....

Table of Contents.

Chapter 1, Tequila	p.6
Chapter 2, Gin	p.12
Chapter 3, Wine	p.19
Chapter 4, Scotch	p.20
Chapter 5, Cognac	p.22
Chapter 6,Brandy	p.23
Chapter 7,Champagne	p.26
Chapter 8.Whiskey	p.28
Chapter 9,Schnapps	p.34
Chapter 10,Rum	p.36
Chapter 11,Liqueur	p.45
Chapter 12,Vodka	p.56
Dictionary	p.71
Notable Liqueur's	p.75
Glasses	p.81
Techniques	p.86
Glossary	p.91

CHAPTER 1, TEQUILA SPIRITS.

Bloody Maria

1 oz. Tequila

Bloody Mary Mix

Garnish with Lime or Celery

Brave Bull

1 oz. Tequila

1/2 oz. Kahlua

Cadillac Margarita

1 oz. 1800 Tequila

1/2 oz. Contreau
Splash of Lime Juice,　　Sour Mix.　　1/2 oz. Grand Mariner Over Top.　　Squeeze Lime (Hang Wheel)
Salt Rim

Double Gold

1 oz.   Jose Cuervo Gold Tequila

1/2 oz.   Goldschlager

Hot Bomb

1 oz.   Tequila

1/2 oz. Cinnamon Schnapps

Mexican Berry

1/2 oz. Tequila

1/2 oz. Chambord

Strawberry Margarita

1 oz. Tequila

1/2 oz. Triple Sec.

Strawberry Mix   Sour Mix

Sugar Rim   Garnish with Strawberry

Tequila Sunrise

1 oz. Tequila

Orange Juice

Top and Float Grenadine

Traditional Margarita

1 oz. Tequila

1/2 oz. Triple Sec

Splash of Lime juice   Sour Mix

Squeeze Lime (Hang Wheel)   Salt Rim

Margarita Madras

1 oz.   Tequila

1/2 oz. Triple Sec

Sour Mix, Orange & Cranberry Juice

Sugar Rim   Garnish with Orange

Gold Margarita

1 oz. Gold Tequila

1/2 oz. Triple Sec

Splash of Lime Juice, Sour Mix

(Wedge / Hang Wheel)

Salt Rim Squeeze Lime

Italian Margarita

1 oz. Tequila

1/2 oz. Amaretto

Sour Mix

Salt Rim

Garnish with Lime Wheel

Mexican Coffee

1 oz. Tequila

Coffee with Whipped Cream

Fuzzy Rita

1 oz. Tequila

1/2 oz. Triple Sec

Orange Juice , Sour Mix

Sugar Rim   Garnish with Orange

Grand Margarita

1 oz. Tequila.

1/2 oz. Grand Marnier

Splash of Lime Juice.   Sour Mix

Squeeze Lime (Hang Wheel)

Salt Rim

Naked Lady

1 oz. Tequila

1/2 oz. Triple Sec

Splash of Lime Juice   Sour Mix

Squeeze Lime (Wedge/ Hang wheel)

Cool Citron

1 oz. Citron Vodka

1/2 oz. White Creme de Menthe

CHAPTER 2, GIN SPIRITS.

Canadian Coffee

1 oz. Seagrams VO

Coffee with Whipped Cream

Dry Martini

2 oz. Gin

Less Dash of Dry Vermouth

Garnish with Olive

Dirty Martini

2 oz. Gin

Dash of Dry Vermouth

Garnish with Olive & Olive Juice

Desert Dry Martini

2 oz. Gin

Dry Vermouth (Toss!)

Garnish with Olive

Extra Dry Martini

2 oz. Gin

Just a Couple Drops of Dry Vermouth

Garnish with Olive

Sloe Gin Fizz

1 oz. Sloe Gin

Sour Mix   Club Soda

Garnish with Cherry

Martini

2 oz. Gin

Dash of Dry Vermouth

Garnish with Olive

Singapore Sling

1 1/2 oz. Gin

1/2 oz. Grenadine

Sour Mix   Fill with Club Soda

Splash of Cherry Brandy

Garnish with Flag

Silver Bullet

1 oz. Gin

Splash of Scotch

Tom Collins

1 oz. Gin

Sour Mix

Splash of Club Soda

Gimlet

1 1/2 oz. Gin

Roses Lime Juice

Garnish with Lime

Sloe Brandy

1/2 oz. Sloe Gin

1 oz. Brandy

Sour Mix

Garnish with Cherry

Sloe Screw

1 oz. Sloe Gin

Orange Juice

French 75

1/2 oz. Gin

Sour Mix

Champagne

Gin Tonic

1 oz. Gin

Tonic Water

Garnish with Lime Wedge

Gibson

2 oz. Gin

Dash of Dry Vermouth

Garnish with Onion

7 & 7

1 oz. Seagram 7

7-up or Sprite

Hal & Half   Martini

1 oz. Gin & 1 oz. Vodka

Dash of Dry Vermouth

Garnish with Lemon Twist

Sloe Comfortable Screw

1/2 oz. Sloe Gin

1/2 oz. Southern Comfort

Orange Juice

Sloe Comfortable Screw up against the Wall

1/2 oz. Sloe Gin

1/2 oz. Southern Comfort

Orange Juice

Float Galliano on Top

CHAPTER 3, WINE SPIRITS.

Spritzer

White Wine

Club Soda

Wine Cooler

White, Red or Rose Wine

Sprite or 7-up

Kir

1 oz. Chambord

White Wine

CHAPTER 4. SCOTCH SPIRITS.

Scotch and Soda

1 oz. Scotch

Club Soda

Godfather

1 oz. Scotch

1/2 oz. Amaretto

Scotch Sour

1 oz. Scotch

Sour Mix

Garnish with Flag

Rob Roy

2 oz. Scotch

Dash of Sweet Vermouth

Garnish with Cherry

Rusty Nail or Nail Driver

1 oz. Scotch

1/2 oz. Drambuie

CHAPTER 5, COGNAC SPIRITS.

French Coffee

1 oz. Cognac

Coffee with Whipped Cream

French 75

1 oz. Cognac

Splash Sour Mix

1/2   tsp. Sugar

Champagne

CHAPTER 6, BRANDY SPIRITS.

Dirty Mother

1 oz. Brandy

1/2 oz. Kahlua

Stinger

1 oz. Brandy

1/2 oz. White Creme de Menthe

God Child

1 oz. Brandy

1/2 oz. Amaretto

Jack Rose Cocktail

1 oz. Apple Jack Brandy

Sour Mix

Grenadine

Italian Stinger

1 oz. Brandy

1/2 oz. Galliano

Iron Cross

1 oz. Rumple Minze

1/2 oz. Apricort Brandy

Side Car

1 oz. Brandy

1/2 oz. Triple Sec.

Sour Mix

(Replace Triple Sec w/Cointreau, put Brandy as shot)
Sugar Rim

CHAPTER 7, CHAMPAGNE SPIRITS.

Champagne Cocktail

1 tbs. Sugar   Champagne

Dash of Bitters

Cilver Citron

1 oz. Absolut Citron

Champagne

Kir Royal

1 oz. Chambord

Champagne

Mimosa

1/4 glass Orange Juice

Champagne

CHAPTER 8, WHISKEY SPIRITS.

Turkey Shooter

White Creme de Menthe

1 oz.   Bourbon

Bloody Molly

1 oz. Irish Whiskey

Bloody Mary Mix

Garnish with Lime or Celery

Surprise

1 oz. Irish Whiskey

Triple Sec

Sour Mix   Garnish with Flag

Boston Eight

1 oz. Bourbon Whiskey

Sour Mix Top with Grenadine

Garnish with Lime Wedge

CC & Soda

1 oz. Canadian Whiskey

Club Soda

Manhattan

2 oz. Whiskey

Dash of Sweet Vermouth

Garnish with Cherry

Nutty Irishman

1 oz. Irish Whiskey

1/2 oz. Frangelico

Coffee with Whipped Cream

Snake Bite

1 oz. Wild Turkey

1/2 oz. Peppermint Schnapps

Southern Sour

1 oz. Bourbon Whiskey

1/2 oz. Southern Comfort

Sour Mix

Garnish with Flag

Whiskey & Water

1 oz. Whiskey

Water

Whiskey Sour

1 oz. Whiskey

Sour Mix

Garnish with Flag

Lynchburg Lemonade

1 oz. Jack Daniels Whiskey

1/2 oz. Triple Sec

Sour Mix

Garnish with Lemon

Jack & Coke

1 oz. Jack Daniels Whiskey

Coke

John Collins

1 oz. Whiskey

Sour Mix

Splash of Club Soda

Irish Sour

1 oz. Irish Whiskey

1 tsp. Sugar

Sour Mix

Garnish with Flag

Irish Coffee #2

1 oz. Irish Whiskey

1/2 oz. Baileys Irish Cream

Coffee with Whipped Cream

Stone Sour

1 oz. Whiskey

Orange Juice   Sour Mix

Garnish with Flag

Scarlet O'Hara

1 oz. Southern Comfort

Sour Mix   Grenadine

Garnish with Flag

CHAPTER 9, SCHNAPPS SPIRITS.

Brain

Peach Schnapps

Drop by Drop Baileys Irish Cream

Juicy Fruit

1/2 oz. Peach Schnapps

1/2 oz. Vodka

1/2 oz.   Midori

Pineapple Juice

Garnish with Flag

Fuzzy Navel

1 oz. Peach Schnapps

Orange Juice

Hot Scotch

1 oz. Butterscotch Schnapps

Coffee with Whipped Cream

Green Chili

1 oz.   Peach Schnapps

1/2 oz. Midori

Tabasco

German Coffee

1 oz. Peppermint Schnapps

Coffee with Whipped Cream

CHAPTER 10, RUM SPIRITS.

Sweet Martini

2 oz. Light Rum

Dash of Sweet Vermouth

Garnish with Cherry

Dry Martini

2 oz. Light Rum

Dash of Dry Vermouth

Garnish with Olive

Rum Cocktail

1 oz. Rum

Sour Mix

Top with Grenadine

Cuba Libra

1 oz. Rum

Coke

Garnish with Lime Wedge

Caribbean Coffee

1 oz. Spiced Rum

Coffee with Whipped Cream

Rum Sour

1 oz.   Spiced Rum

1 tsp. Sugar

Sour Mix

Garnish with Flag

Daiquiri

1 oz. Light Rum

Sour Mix

Garnish with Flag

Mai Tai

1 oz. Rum

1/2 oz. Triple Sec

1/2 oz. Almond Syrup

Grenadine

Sour Mix, Garnish with Flag

Skip & Go Naked

1/2 oz. Light Rum

1/2 oz. Vodka

1/2 oz. Brandy   Sour Mix

Splash Orange Juice, Splash of Grenadine

The Eraser

1/2 oz. 151 Rum

1/2 oz   Blackberry Brandy

Cranberry Juice

Rum & Coke

1 oz. Rum

Coke

Electric Lemonade

1/2 oz. Rum

1/2 oz. Vodka

1/2 oz. Gin

1/2 oz. Tequila

1/2 oz. Triple Sec

Sour Mix ,Top with Sprite   Garnish with Lemon

Green Dinosaur

1/2 oz. Rum

1/2 oz. Vodka

1/2 oz. Gin

1/2 oz. Tequila

1/2 oz. Trip Sec

Sour Mix

Top with Midori   Garnish with Lemon

Long Beach Tea

1/2 oz. Rum

1/2 oz. Vodka

1/2 oz. Gin

1/2 oz. Tequila

1/2 oz. Triple Sec.

Sour Mix, Top with Cranberry juice

Garnish with Lemon
Malibu Suntan

1 oz. Malibu Rum

Iced Tea

Garnish with Lemon

Long Island Ice Tea

1/2 oz. Rum

1/2 oz. Vodka

1/2 oz. Gin

1/2 oz.   Tequila

1/2 oz. Triple sec

Sour Mix, Top with Coke   Garnish with Lemon.

Heat Wave

1 oz. Rum

1/2 oz. Peach Schnapps

Pineapple Juice   Splash of Grenadine

Garnish with Flag
Hurricane

1 oz. Light Rum

1oz. Dark Rum

1/2 oz. Grenadine

Passion Fruit

Sour Mix

Garnish with Flag

Rum Runner

1/2 oz. Lt. Rum

1/2 oz. Blackberry Brandy

1/2 oz. Creme de Banana

1/2 oz. Grenadine

Sour Mix, Float a Little Dark Rum or 151

Zombie

1/2 oz. Light Rum

1/2 oz. Dark Rum

1/2 oz. Amaretto

1/2 oz. Triple Sec

Sour Mix, Splash of Orange Juice, Float 151 Rum on Top.

Garnish with Flag

Blue Hawaiian

1 oz. Rum

1/2 oz. Blue Curacao

Pineapple Juice

Garnish with Cherry

Flaming Dr. Pepper

1 oz. 151 Rum in shot Glass.

Float Amaretto over top

Light and Drop Shooter in 1/2 Glass of Lite Beer.

CHAPTER 11, LIQUEUR SPIRITS.

French Tickler

1 oz. Goldschlager

1/2 oz. Grand Marinier

B-52

1/2 oz. Baileys Irish Cream

1/2 oz. Kahlua

1/2 oz. Grand Marinier

Buttery Finger

1/2 oz. Vodka

1/2 oz. Kahlua

1/2 oz. Butterscotch Schnapps

1/2 oz. Baileys Irish Cream
Bubble Gum

1/2 oz. Creme de Banana

1/2 oz. Midori

1/2 oz. Vodka

Grenadine

Orange Juice

Baileys & Coffee

1 oz. Baileys Irish Cream

Coffee with Whipped Cream

Cafe Nelson

1/2 oz. Kahlua

1/2 oz. Baileys Irish Cream

1/2 oz. Frangelico

Coffee with Whipped Cream

Chambord Iceberg

1/2 oz. Chambord

1 oz. Vodka

Dirty Girl Scout Cookie

1 oz. Baileys Irish Cream

1/2 oz. Creme de Menthe

Dirty Harry

1 oz. Grand Marnier

1/2 oz. Tia Maria

Millionaire's Coffee

1/2 oz. Grand Marnier

1/2 oz. Kahlua

1/2 oz. Baileys Irish Cream

Coffee with Whipped Cream
Slippery Nipple

1 oz. Sambuca

1/2 oz. Peach Schnapps

Slippery Nut

1/2 oz.   Frangelico

1 oz. Baileys Irish Cream

Sex on the Beach Shot

1/2 oz. Chambord

1/2 oz. Midori

1/2 oz. Vodka

Pineapple Juice

Irish Coffee #1

1 oz. Irish Coffee

Coffee with Whipped Cream

Top with Green Creme de Menthe

Toasted Almond

1 oz. Amaretto

1/2 oz. Kahlua

Cream (1/2 & 1/2) or Milk

Galliano Stinger

1 oz. Tia Maria

Coffee with Whipped Cream

International Stinger

1 oz. Galliano

1/2 oz.   White Creme de Menthe

Italian Coffee

1 oz. Galliano

Coffee with Whipped Cream

Sombrero

1 oz. Kahlua

Cream (1/2 & 1/2) or Milk

Scotch Coffee

1 oz. Drambuie

Coffee with Whipped Cream

Harbor Lights

1/2 oz. Amaretto

1/2 oz. Brandy

1/2 oz. Kahlua

1/2 oz. Tequila

Greek Coffee

1 oz. Ouzo

Coffee with Whipped Cream

Grand Am

1 oz. Grand Marnier

1/2 oz. Amaretto

Gold Furnace

1 1/2 oz. Goldschlager

Tabasco

Good & Plenty

1 oz. Kahlua

1 oz. Ouzo

Girl Scout Cookie

1 oz. Brown Creme de Cacao

1 oz. White Creme de Menthe

Cream

Wet Spot

1/2 oz. Baileys Irish Cream

1 oz. Tequila

Grasshopper

1/2 oz. Green Creme de Menthe

1/2 oz. White Creme de Cacao

Cream (1/2 & 1/2) or Milk

Cross Sip Stick

Orgasm

1 oz. Kahlua

1 oz. Baileys Irish Cream

1/2 oz. Frangelico

Oatmeal Cookie

1/2 oz. Baileys Irish Cream

1/2 oz. Butterscotch Schnapps

1/2 oz. Goldschlager

Baileys Chocolate Covered Cherry

1 oz. Baileys Irish Cream

Grenadine

1/2 oz. Kahlua

(Can also layer)

CHAPTER 12, VODKA SPIRITS.

Woo Woo

1oz. Vodka

1/2 oz. Peach Schnapps

Cranberry Juice

Bay Breeze

1 oz. Vodka

Cranberry Juice

Pineapple Juice

Garnish with Lime

Bloody Mary

1 oz. Vodka

Bloody Mary Mix

Garnish with Lime or Celery

Cajun Martini

2 oz. Pepper Vodka

Dry Vermouth

Salt Rim

Citron Martini

2 oz. Citrus Vodka

Dash of Dry Vermouth

Sugar Rim with Lemon

Cape Codder

1 oz. Vodka

Cranberry Juice

Garnish with Lime

Citron Cooler

1 oz. Citron Vodka

Sour Mix

Tonic Water

Garnish with Lime Wedge

Emerald Vodka Martini

2 oz. Vodka

Splash of Midori

Dash of Dry Vermouth

Garnish with Lime

Sex on the Beach

1/2 oz. Vodka

1/2 oz. Midori

1/2 oz. Peach Schnapps, Cranberry Juice

Splash of Pineapple Juice

Madras

1 oz. Vodka

Cranberry Juice

Orange Juice

Garnish with Lime

Nutty Martini

1 oz. Vodka

1 oz. Frangelico
or
1 oz. Amaretto

Nuts & Berry's

1 oz. Vodka

1/2 oz. Creme de almond

Cream (1/2 & 1/2) or Milk

Nervous Breakdown

1 oz. Vodka

1/2 oz. Chambord

Cranberry Juice

Splash of Club Soda

Screaming Orgasm Against the Wall

1 oz. Vodka

1/2 oz. Galliano

Cream

Silver Bullet

1 oz. Vodka

Splash of Scotch

Sweet Tart

1/2 oz. Vodka

1/2 oz. Chambord

1/2 oz. Midori

Sour Mix

Tootsie Roll

1/2 oz. Vodka

1 oz. Kahlua

Orange Juice

Vodka Martini

2 oz. Vodka

Dash of Dry Vermouth

Garnish with Olive

Vodka Tonic

1 oz. Vodka

Tonic Water

Garnish with Lime Wedge

Razz Ma Tazz

1 oz. Vodka

1/2 oz. Chambord

Club Soda

Golden Day

1 oz. Vodka

1/2 oz. Galliano

Godmother

1 oz. Vodka

1/2 oz. Amaretto

Kamakazi

1 1/2 oz. Vodka

Triple Sec ,Lime Juice

(Some prefer Sour mix too)

Garnish with Lime

Killer Kool Aid

1/2 oz. Vodka

1/2 oz. Gin

1/2 oz. Rum

1/2 oz. Chambord

Sour Mix   Top with Club Soda

Sea Breeze

1 oz. Vodka

Cranberry Juice

Grapefruit Juice

Garnish with Lime

Salty Dog

1 oz. Vodka

Grapefruit Juice

Salt Rim

Screwdriver

1 oz. Vodka

Orange Juice

4th of July

Blue Curacao

1 oz. Vodka

Grenadine

Fool's Gold

1 oz. Vodka

1/2 oz. Galliano

Green Hornet

1 oz. Vodka

1/2 oz. Midori

Sour Mix

Greyhound

1 oz. Vodka

Grapefruit Juice

Gremlin

1 oz. Vodka

1/2 oz. Blue Curacao

1/2 oz. Rum

Orange Juice

Garnish with Orange Slice

Real Gold

1 oz. Vodka

1/2 oz. Goldschlager

Roasted Almond

1 oz. Amaretto

1/2 oz. Vodka

Cream (1/2 & 1/2) or Milk

White Russian

1 oz. Vodka

1/2 oz. Kahlua

Cream (1/2 & 1/2) or Milk

Watermelon

1 oz Vodka

1/2 oz. Midori

Cranberry Juice

Mudslide

1 oz. Vodka

1/2 oz. Baileys Irish Cream

1/2 oz. Kahlua

Midnight Martini

1 1/2 oz. Vodka

1/2 oz. Chambord

Garnish with Lemon Twist

Hairy Navel

1/2 oz. Peach Schnapps

1/2 oz. Vodka

Orange Juice

Lemon Drop

1 oz. Vodka

Triple Sec, Splash of Sour Mix

Squeeze 1/2 Lemon

Sugar, Garnish with Lemon

Buttery Nipple

1/2 oz. Vodka

1/2 oz. Butterscotch Schnapps

1/2 oz. Baileys Irish Cream

Cosmopolitan Martini

1 oz. Vodka

1/2 oz. Cointreau

3 Dashes of Lime & Cranberry Juice

Garnish with Lemon Twist

Hot Pants

1 oz. Pepper Vodka

1/2 oz. Peach Schnapps

Grape Crush

1 oz. Vodka

1/2 oz. Black Raspberry Schnapps

Sour Mix

7-up

Dictionary

Brandy - A potable spirit, distilled from a fermented mash of grapes or other fruit. Most brandy is distilled from wine. White wine, made from white grapes, is used most often. Wine that has recently finished its fermentation process makes the best brandy. An aged wine, even if it is of superior quality, won't make a good brandy.

Champagne - A sparkling white wine made from a blend of grapes, especially Chardonnay and pinot, produced in Champagne.

Garnish - A decoration or embellishment for your drink. ie. Olive, Lemon etc.

Gin- A spirit distilled from grain that receives its unique flavor and aroma from juniper berries and other botanicals. Every gin producer has his own special recipe, which is under strict quality control. The flavor of gin will vary with the distiller. Gin was first produced in Holland by Dr. Sylvius, a Dutch physician, during the 17th century. He named it Genievre, the French word for the juniper berry. It was the English who shortened the name to gin. Brought from Holland into England by English soldiers, who called it "Dutch Courage", gin soon became the national drink of England and has so remained.

Flag - Flags are garnishes that skewer a maraschino cherry on top of another garnish, such as an orange slice or pineapple wedge. Think of the cherry as a flag being planted on top of the other garnish.

Liqueurs - The words liqueurs and cordials are used interchangeably. Liqueurs were first developed by the Christian monks of the middle ages. They were developed to help the sick. The monks added secret combinations of honey, seeds, herbs, spices, roots, and bark to distilled-base spirits and offered them as remedies.

Rum - A spirit produced wherever sugar cane grows. Many countries, such as the United States, South Africa, and even Russia, produce rum, but it is only the

Caribbean Islands that produce rum in quantities sufficient for worldwide export. The islands in the Caribbean each produce a distinctive type of rum, the result of the base material used, the method of distillation, and the length of maturation. Generally, the islands where the Spanish language is spoken, such as Puerto Rico, produce light, dry-tasting rums. The English speaking Caribbean islands produce dark, heavy-tasting rums.

Tequila - the primary spirit of Mexico, has its own special flavor that is almost tart and leaves the tongue clean and tingling. In the 1970s, tequila became the fastest growing spirit in sales, as vodka did in the 1960s. Tequila is obtained from the distillation of the fermented juice (sap) of the mescal plant, called pulque. The only source for Tequila is the mescal plant, which is a species of the agave plant. It is a cactus that takes between twelve and thirteen years to mature. Its long leaves, or spikes, are cut off at harvest time, leaving only the bulbous central core, called the pina, meaning pineapple. The pinas, which weigh from 80 pounds to 175 pounds each are taken to the distillery where they are cooked in pressure cookers for several hours. They are then cooled and shredded, and the juice is pressed out. The fermentation process is completed in huge wooden vats. The fermented juice is then twice distilled in traditional copper-pot stills.

Vodka - Like whiskey, vodka is distilled from a fermented mash of grain, but they differ in the methods of distillation. Whiskey is distilled at a low proof to retain flavor. Vodka, however, is distilled at a high proof, 190 or above, and then processed even further to remove all flavor. Most American distillers filter their vodkas through activated charcoal. Also, whiskey is aged, and vodka is not.

Whiskey - A spirit, aged in wood, obtained from the distillation of a fermented mash of grain. Whiskey is produced in the United States, Canada, Scotland, and Ireland. The whiskeys produced in Canada, Ireland, and Scotland take on the name of their countries.

Wine - An alcoholic drink made from fermented grape juice.

Notable Liqueur's

After Shock - Cinnamon liqueur imported from Canada. Initially tastes like hot cinnamon.

Amaretto Di Saronno - Imported Italian liqueur made from apricot stones, which produce an almond flavor.

B & B D.O.M. - Imported liqueur from France. A combination of Benedictine and Brandy that started out as a popular mixed drink until the French decided to bottle the two together.

Campari Aperitivo - Aperitif imported from Italy. Aromas of fruit pits and botanicals. Slightly bitter flavors of fruit.

Chambord - Black raspberry liqueur from France made with small black raspberries, other fruits, herbs and honey.

Chartreuse Green - Herbal liqueur made by the monks of the Carthusian order in the French Alps.

Cointreau Liqueur - Imported orange liqueur from France. Similar to orange curacao. Clear in color. Flavor of fresh orange peels with a slight hint of spice.

Romana Black Sambuca - Imported licorice flavored liqueur from Italy. Black color.

Drambuie - Imported liqueur from Scotland. Made with aged Scotch-over 15 years old-and blended with heather honey and herbs.

Frangelico - Hazelnut Liqueur imported from Italy. A mix of hazelnuts, berries, and herbs. Flavors of hazelnut and butter.

Goldschlager - Clear cinnamon schnapps from Switzerland with flakes of gold leaf floating in the bottle. Sweet-sour cinnamon flavors.

Grand Marnier - Made with cognac, essence of wild oranges and delicate syrup, the mixture is aged in oak casks prior to bottling.

Irish Mist Liqueur - Imported liqueur from Ireland. A blend of heather and clover honey and herbs.

Jagermeister -   Imported liqueur from Germany. Intensely herbal, citrus nose.

Liquore Galliano - Imported liqueur from Italy. Aromas of roots, herbs, flowers, and cedar.

Metaxa Ouzo - Imported liqueur from Greece. A combination of grapes, herbs, and berries including aniseed, licorice, mint, wintergreen, fennel, and hazelnut.

Pernod Anise - The recipe for Pernod is a slight variation of the original recipe for absinthe; an herbal elixer made from 15 exotic herbs steeped in alcohol. Licorice flavored and yellow-green color.

Midori Melon - Imported honeydew melon flavored liqueur. Light, fresh melon taste.

Yukon Jack - Canadian liqueur. White-wine-like appearance. Flavors of orange and spirit.

Kahlua Coffee Liqueur- America's number one imported liqueur. Aromas of coffee beans. Flavors of coffee and semisweet chocolate.

Tia Maria Coffee Liqueur - *Imported coffee liqueur from Jamaica.*

Bailey's Irish Cream - *Cream liqueur imported from Ireland. A blend of real cream and Irish whiskey.*

Melon Liqueur - *Sweet melon flavored.*

Brown Creme De Cacao - *Brown color. Rich cocoa flavor.*

White Creme De Cacao - *Clear color, taste the same as the Brown Crème De Cacao.*

Creme De Menthe Green - *Dark green color. Mint flavor.*

White Creme De Menthe - *Clear. Natural mint flavor.*

Creme De Banana - *American banana flavored liqueur. The 'Creme' means that this liqueur is sweeter than most liqueurs or schnapps, not that it is blended with cream.*

Creme De Noyaux - *Made from fruit stones (pits) that gives it a nutty, almond flavor. Similar in flavor to Crème De Almond.*

Creme De Cassis - Black currant flavored liqueur.

Peppermint Schnapps - Peppermint flavored liqueur. Schnapps is less sweet than a liqueur or a fruit creme.

Peach Schnapps - Peach flavored. Most schnapps are generally low in proof and contain a lower sugar content than other cordials.

Root Beer Schnapps - Root Beer flavored schnapps made in the U.S.
Buttershots Schnapps - Cordial that has intense butterscotch aromas and flavors.

Fire Water Cinnamon Schnapps - Hot cinnamon schnapps, like fireball candy. 100 proof.

Anisette - American liqueur with the aroma and flavor of licorice from the anise seed.

Orange Curacao - Orange flavored (only natural ingredients are used) liqueur. Made from orange peel.

Blue Curacao - Orange flavored. Made from orange peel. Blue color.

Triple Sec - Orange flavored liqueur. Orange peels are used for the flavoring. Similar to curacao, but more refined.

Southern Comfort - A blend of bourbon and peach liqueur. Made from bourbon and peach liqueur in which fresh peaches were marinated.

Glasses

Beer mug-
The traditional beer container.
Typical Size: 16 oz.

Brandy snifter
The shape of this glass concentrates the alcoholic odors to the top of the glass as your hands warm the brandy.
Typical Size: 17.5 oz.

Champagne flute-
This tulip shaped glass is designed to show off the waltzing bubbles of the wine as they brush against the side of the glass and spread out into a sparkling mousse.
Typical Size: 6 oz.

Cocktail glass-
This glass has a triangle-bowl design with a long stem, and is used for a wide range of straight-up (without ice) cocktails, including martinis, manhattans, metropolitans, and gimlets. Also known as a martini glass.
Typical Size: 4-12 oz.

Coffee mug-
The traditional mug used for hot coffee.
Typical Size: 12-16 oz.

Collins glass-
Shaped similarly to a highball glass, only taller, the collins glass was originally used for the line of collins gin drinks, and is now also commonly used for soft drinks, alcoholic juice, and tropical/exotic juices such as Mai Tai's.
Typical Size: 14 oz.

Cordial glass-
Small and stemmed glasses used for serving small portions of your favourite liquors at times such as after a meal.
Typical Size: 2 oz.

Highball glass-
A straight-sided glass, often an elegant way to serve many types of mixed drinks, like those served on the rocks, shots, and mixer combined liquor drinks (ie. gin and tonic).
Typical Size: 8-12 oz.

Hurricane glass-
A tall, elegantly cut glass named after it's hurricane-lamp-like shape, used for exotic/tropical drinks.
Typical Size: 15 oz.

Margarita/coupette glass-
This slightly larger and rounded approach to a cocktail glass has a broad-rim for holding salt, ideal for margarita's. It is also used in daiquiris and other fruit drinks.
Typical Size: 12 oz.

Mason jar-
These large square containers are effective in keeping their contents sealed in an air tight environment. They're designed for home canning, being used for preserves and jam amongst other things.
Typical Size: 16 oz.

Old-fashioned glass-
A short, round so called "rocks" glass, suitable for cocktails or liquor served on the rocks, or "with a splash".
Typical Size: 8-10 oz.

Parfait glass-
This glass has a similar inwards curve to that of a hurricane glass, with a steeper outwards rim and larger, rounded bowl. Often used for drinks containing fruit or ice cream.
Typical Size: 12 oz.

Pousse-cafe glass-
A narrow glass essentially used for pousse café's and other layered dessert drinks. It's shape increases the ease of layering ingredients.
Typical Size: 6 oz.

Punch bowl-
A large demispherical bowl suitable for punches or large mixes.
Typical Size: 1-5 gal.

Red wine glass-
A clear, thin, stemmed glass with a round bowl tapering inward at the rim.
Typical Size: 8 oz.

Sherry glass-
The preferred glass for aperitifs, ports, and sherry. The copita, with it's aroma enhancing narrow taper, is a type of sherry glass.
Typical Size: 2 oz.

Shot glass-
A small glass suitable for vodka, whiskey and other liquors. Many "shot" mixed drinks also call for shot glasses.
Typical Size: 1.5 oz.

Whiskey sour glass-
Also known as a delmonico glass, this is a stemmed, wide opening glass, alike to a small version of a champagne flute.
Typical Size: 5 oz.

White wine glass-
A clear, thin, stemmed glass with an elongated oval bowl tapering inward at the rim.
Typical Size: 12.5 oz.

Techniques

Shaking

When a drink contains eggs, fruit juices or cream, it is necessary to shake the ingredients. Shaking is the method by which you use a cocktail shaker to mix ingredients together and chill them simultaneously. The object is to almost freeze the drink whilst breaking down and combining the ingredients. Normally this is done with ice cubes three-quarters of the way full. When you've poured in the ingredients, hold the shaker in both hands, with one hand on top and one supporting the base, and give a short, sharp, snappy shake. It's important not to rock your cocktail to sleep. When water has begun to condense on the surface of the shaker, the cocktail should be sufficiently chilled and ready to be strained.

Straining

Most cocktail shakers are sold with a build-in strainer or hawthorn strainer. When a drink calls for straining, ensure you've used ice cubes, as crushed ice tends to clog the strainer of a standard shaker. If indeed a drink is required shaken with crushed ice (ie. Shirley Temple), it is to be served unstrained.

Stirring

You can stir cocktails effectively with a metal or glass rod in a mixing glass. If ice is to be used, use ice cubes to prevent dilution, and strain the contents into a glass when the surface of the mixing glass begins to collect condensation.

Muddling

To extract the most flavor from certain fresh ingredients such as fruit or mint garnishes, you should crush the ingredient with the muddler on the back end of your bar spoon, or with a pestle.

Blending

An electric blender is needed for recipes containing fruit or other ingredients which do not break down by shaking. Blending is an appropriate way of combining these ingredients with others, creating a smooth ready to serve mixture. Some recipes will call for ice to be placed in the blender, in which case you would use a suitable amount of crushed ice.

Building

When building a cocktail, the ingredients are poured into the glass in which the cocktail will be served. Usually, the ingredients are floated on top of each other, but occasionally, a swizzle stick is put in the glass, allowing the ingredients to be mixed.

Layering

To layer or float an ingredient (ie. cream, liqueurs) on top of another, use the rounded or back part of a spoon and rest it against the inside of a glass. Slowly pour down the spoon and into the glass. The ingredient should run down the inside of the glass and remain seperated from the ingredient below it. Learning the approximate weight of certain liqueurs and such will allow you to complete this technique more successfully, as lighter ingredients can then be layered on top of heavier ones.

Flaming

Flaming is the method by which a cocktail or liquor is set alight, normally to enhance the flavor of a drink. It should only be attempted with caution, and for the above reason only, not to simply look cool.

Some liquors will ignite quite easily if their proof is high. Heating a small amount of the liquor in a spoon will cause the alcohol to collect at the top, which can then be easily lit. You can then pour this over the prepared ingredients. Don't add alcohol to ignited drinks, don't leave them unattended, light them where they pose no danger to anybody else, and ensure no objects can possibly come into contact with any flames from the drink. Always extinguish a flaming drink before consuming it.

Glossary

Chapter 1, Tequila Spirits.

Bloody Maria

Brave Maria

Cadillac Margarita

Cool Citron

Double Gold

Fuzzy Rita

Gold Margarita

Grand Margarita

Hot Bomb

Italian Margarita

Margarita Madras

Mexican Berry

Mexican Coffee

Naked Lady

Strawberry Margarita

Tequila Sunrise

Traditional Margarita

Chapter 2, Gin Spirits.

7 & 7

Canadian Coffee

Desert Dry Martini

Dry Martini

Dirty Martini

Extra Dry Martini

French 75

Gibson

Gin Tonic

Gimlet

Half & Half Martini

Martini

Singapore Sling

Silver Bullet

Sloe Gin Fizz

Sloe Brandy

Sloe Screw

Sloe Comfortable Screw

Sloe Comfortable Screw Up Against the Wall.

Tom Collins

Chapter 3, Wine Spirits.

Kir

Spritzer

Wine Cooler

Chapter 4, Scotch Spirits.

Godfather

Nail Driver

Scotch Sour

Scotch & Soda

Rob Roy

Rusty Nail

Chapter 5, Cognac Spirits.

French 75

French Coffee

Chapter 6, Brandy Spirits.

Dirty Mother

God Child

Italian Stinger

Iron Cross

Jack Rose

Side Car

Stinger

Chapter 7, Champagne Spirits.

Champagne Cocktail

Cilver Citron

Kir Cocktail

Mimosa

Chapter 8, Whiskey Spirits.

Bloody Molly

Boston Eight

CC & Soda

Irish Sour

Irish Coffee #2

Jack & Coke

John Collins

Lynchburg Lemonade

Manhattan

Nutty Irishman

Scarlet O'hara

Snake Bite

Southern Sour

Stone Sour

Surprise

Turkey Shooter

Whiskey Sour

Whiskey & Water

Chapter 9, Schnapps Spirits.

Brain

Fuzzy Navel

Hot Scotch

Juicy Fruit

German Coffee

Green Chili

Chapter 10, Rum Spirits.

Blue Hawaiian

Caribbean Coffee

Cuba Libra

Daiquiri

Dry Martini

Electric Lemonade

Flaming Dr. Pepper

Green Dinosaur

Heat Wave

Hurricane

Long Beach Tea

Long Island Ice Tea

Mai Tai

Malibu Suntan

Rum Cocktail

Rum Sour

Rum & Coke

Rum Runner

Skip and Go Naked

Sweet Martini

The eraser

Zombie

Chapter 11, Liqueur Spirits.

B-52

Baileys & Coffee

Baileys Chocolate Covered Cherry

Bubble Gum

Buttery Finger

Cafe Nelson

Chambord Iceberg

Dirty Harry

Dirty Girl Scout Cookie

French Tickler

Galliano Stinger

Girl Scout Cookie

Gold Furnace

Good & Plenty

Grass Hopper

Grand Am

Greek Coffee

Harbor Lights

International Stinger

Italian Coffee

Irish Coffee #1

Millionaire's Coffee

Orgasm

Oatmeal Cookie

Scotch Coffee

Sex on the Beach shot

Slippery Nipple

Slippery Nut

Sumbrero

Toasted Almond

Wet Spot

Chapter 12, Vodka Spirits.

4th of July

Bay Breeze

Bloody Mary

Buttery Nipple

Cape Codder

Cajun Martini

Citron Martini

Citron Cooler

Cosmopolitan Martini

Emerald Vodka Martini

Fool's Gold

Golden Day

Godmother

Green Hornet

Greyhound

Gremlin

Grape Crush

Hairy Navel

Hot Pants

Kamakazi

Killer Kool Aid

Lemon Drop

Madras

Midnight Martini

Mud Slide

Nervous Breakdown

Nutty Martini

Nuts & Berry's

Razz Ma Tazz

Real Gold

Roasted Almond

Salty Dog

Sea Breeze

Screaming Orgasm Against the Wall

Screwdriver

Sex on the Beach

Silver Bullet

Sweet Tart

Tootsie Roll

Vodka Martini

Vodka Tonic

Watermelon

White Russian

Woo Woo

**Read more Printhouse titles available in ebook , Hard cover and paperback.
Tiltles are available on all ereader devices**

and mobile apps. Titles can be purchased at PrintHousebooks.com and everywhere books are sold.

VIP INK Publishing Group, Inc.

PrintHousebooks.com

ANT BANK$

Atlanta, GA.

Dear Reader,

The journey you are about to embark on is about Andy Cooper; a military vet, turned hustler, turned Gangster, turned Crime Boss. His marriage is on the rocks; fresh out of the military, AC finds himself broke and lost with a Wife and three kids to feed. Trapped in Sin City and working any job he can get from day to day, to make ends meet. Hating the state of mind he's in right now, a really fucked up way to be! Gone are the days when Uncle Sam paid for housing, day care and groceries. Now, all own his own again, with no idea of where life is going to take him. One thing for sure, Andy "AC" Cooper no longer wanted to wear that Army uniform another day. Coop loved every minute of it and would not trade it for the world but the next chapter of his life was about to start. It just so happen that he landed in Las Vegas, one of the hardest cities to make it in, it is truly the land of the Hustler. What the outsiders don't know is that beneath the bright neon lights, the delicious buffets and luxurious casino's, lays a whole different world that would eventually suck him in.

Dear Reader,

The word Adoration can be defined as fervent and devoted love or simply put; to worship. During our time on Earth we will all experience this powerful thing called Love. This novel will take you on a journey seen through the eyes of four couples and their relationships. For Love we endure amazing things and some of us will go to the limit to keep it.

Love can fill your heart with joy or leave it filled with hate. Adoration explores love at several levels; some of them good; some bad. In Book One of this Series; hearts will break, tears will fall, blood will shed and bells will chime; all in the name of love.

Dear Reader,

Earlier in the mid 80's and early 90's; I had the unfortunate opportunity of being friends or acquaintances with two special individuals. Now that I am thinking about it, maybe it wasn't unfortunate but faith that we crossed paths. Their stories we're similar, even though they happened at different times and in two separate parts of the world.

It is through my God given gift that I will deliver their message; through Eric; F.I.T.H's main character. I find it my destiny to help others see life as they did; at tragic moments in both their lives. The time and location of events and names have been changed to protect them and their victim's families. Hopefully this story will show why it's not cool to be a bully but deadly, when you factor in all the consequences.

The Cover Girl series is about, an Atlanta; Eye Candy photographer; name Malakhi Jones. Pronounced (*Mal uh Ky).* This short story and many others to come; will take you inside a day in the life of a hot photographer and his daily encounters with several of the industries sexiest Magazine Models and Video Vixens.

While these events are Fiction; anyone in the industry knows; what goes on at the shoot; stays at the shoot! Malakhi is at the top of his game and is connected with every Men's Magazine Publisher, Casting Directors, Hip Hop Artist and Talent Managers in the industry. Getting a session with him is like winning the lottery; when it comes to being an eye candy Model, in the ATL. Any Model knows; that once the session starts and that camera flashes; all rules will be broken to obtain that success; if not! Then keep dreaming.

The Cover Girl Series is only available as an E-short on ebook readers.

PRINTHOUSE BOOKS
Read it; Enjoy it; Tell a friend!

www.ingramcontent.com/pod-product-compliance
Lightning Source LLC
Chambersburg PA
CBHW020012050426
42450CB00005B/441